The Food Truck Startup

Start Your Own Food Truck
Leave the Corporate World Behind!

By Andrew Moorehouse

A Free Gift for You

As a thank you for your purchase, I'm making my book **Food Truck Vehicles and Equipment** available to you for free.

You'll get an introduction to food trucks and the vehicles used in the industry. In this booklet, you can find some basic costs of buying a food truck and learn about what food truck builders can do for you.

Visit the URL below for this exclusive offer:

TheFoodTruckStartup.com/free

Books Available in the
Food Truck Startup Series

Table of Contents

Introduction

The mobile food industry continues to soar to new heights! If you haven't seen a food truck in your city, you will soon! When a food truck shows up in a neighborhood, it drives hordes of people to exit their homes and offices to sample unique and delicious foods. Even the traditional food booths at festivals are starting to be replaced by food trucks. The reason? When a food truck is around, people know that there's tasty food to be found.

While chowing down on some of their favorite meals, a lot of patrons are noticing the incredible income potential of owning a food truck. Today, more and more people are seeing this as an entrepreneurial opportunity. This has led many of the same patrons to leave their boring jobs for one that offers excitement and new challenges every day! Others who have dreamed of opening a restaurant now see a lower barrier to entry thus making their dreams easier to achieve.

Many people who start food trucks come from the corporate world with backgrounds in marketing, sales, public relations, real estate and more. They are taking their business skills and pairing it up with their love of food. Often, they are eventually able to create a new source of sustainable income. Some of the youngest food truck owners haven't even received their diplomas from college yet! But their entrepreneurial spirit has driven them to launch a business that can continue on long after they've graduated.

This book is designed to inspire and introduce you to the fascinating world of the food truck industry. It is for men, women, students, dads, moms and anyone else who has been mesmerized by the popularity of food trucks. Like starting any business, it's going to take a lot of work but it can change your life! Let's get ready to explore the different aspects of what it takes to start your own food truck!

-Andrew Moorehouse

Chapter 1 - The Growing Food Truck Industry!

Starting a business is a dream many of us have! Imagine being your own boss and setting your own hours. You could be making money for yourself and eliminating the long commutes to an unsatisfying and unrewarding job. If the idea of working for yourself sounds appealing, then the food truck industry might be what you're looking for! The food truck industry is growing at an enormous rate and part of that growth is due to the slow economy.

Just about every city in North America has been hit by the gourmet food truck revolution and it appears to be here to stay! Every month, new trucks are being launched from coast to coast. At the end of 2011, the industry tracking website, Mobile-Cuisine.com estimated at least 10 new trucks a month were hitting the streets. That number is much higher now.

These new food trucks specialize in gourmet-style food with unique twists. Forget about the standard hot dogs, burgers and tacos. So boring! These trucks have reinvented classic dishes (and more) into gourmet versions that rival menus from the best restaurants!

Why Food Trucks?

Now it's important to understand why the food truck industry is growing so rapidly. A major part of this growth is a direct result of the poor economy and people losing their jobs. This has led numerous individuals to find new sources of income or even start their own businesses. Consumers are also growing more health conscious so they're looking for healthy alternatives when it comes to food. A growing number of trucks are starting to cater this audience by offering gluten-free and paleo-based dishes. While more trucks are starting to offer healthy alternatives, this is not the norm. Come to think about it, a cheese-stuffed burger with fried bacon and a glazed donut for the bun is not exactly something a health conscious consumer would order!

This huge growth can also be attributed to significantly lower start-up costs than a brick-and-mortar restaurant. This is one of the key motivating factors for starting a food truck. These rolling kitchens can also be relocated easily if business is slow and it requires less staff to operate.

On the other side of the industry are the customers. Good food always attracts people! And when it's good, they love to share their eating experiences. That's because a large part of our social gatherings are based around food. With this basic understanding of people and business, it's clear that the mobile food industry can offer some incredible opportunities for creative entrepreneurs!

Rise of the Food Truck Entrepreneur

So how is it that there are so many entrepreneurs launching new food trucks each and every month? Some have chosen to become entrepreneurs by choice. Others have been thrown into a desperate situation by factors out of their direct control. Everyone has a different reason for starting a food truck. Oftentimes, a food truck is used to expand an existing business (like a restaurant or catering company) or it's a way to create a second income stream for individuals.

Others have started food trucks because they are unemployed or have lost their jobs for one reason or another. More adventurous individuals usually start a food truck because they just want to try something different. They'll actually quit their day jobs to try their hand at running a food truck business full-time. Even well-known food businesses are starting to notice the potential in the mobile food industry. Jack in the Box,

Chipotle, Whole Foods and other well-known national restaurant chains and stores have started their own food trucks to capitalize on their share of this industry.

Even with so many newcomers, the food truck industry continues to grow at an alarming rate! It's a great way to get into the food service business where you can be rewarded for your hard work while gaining the appreciation you deserve!

Chapter 2 - Do You Have What It Takes?

One of the most common questions future food truck owners ask is "How do I get started"? It's great if you have the enthusiasm and drive to start your journey of becoming an entrepreneur but there are a lot of personal questions you need to ask yourself right from the start!

It's a common misconception that the first thing you need is a food truck and some good recipes… that actually comes later in the journey. To prepare yourself to be an owner of a popular, successful food truck, here is a checklist of thoughts and items to consider before you even spend a dime to start your own food truck.

Do you have the start-up budget?
Will there be a return on your investment?
How much time can you commit?
Is this a full-time business?
Is this a part-time business?
Have you owned a business before?
Do you have any cooking skills?
Do you have experience in sales?
Do you have any marketing skills?
How many employees will you hire?

Will you have more trucks in the future?

Can you build a customer base?

Can you sustain your business?

What hours are you open?

Can you find the best locations?

Defining Gourmet Food Trucks

Once you've given some consideration to those ideas, we can move on to define what exactly is a gourmet food truck? The term food truck can be used to describe all mobile food trucks but until recently, there is a clear distinction between the trucks being launched today versus the food trucks of earlier years. The classic food trucks offered standard menus and average food. A lot of them served meals that were already prepared or prepackaged. Some of the classic trucks may have even cooked on-site. The classic taco truck falls into that category. Compare that with today's gourmet food trucks and you'll clearly see the difference. Today's food trucks serve higher quality food. They usually specialize in one type of food or a focused niche. Gourmet food trucks utilize high-tech marketing to get customers to their locations and food is often cooked in the truck for freshness and taste.

Gourmet food trucks also have bright, colorful branding and logos on the exterior panels of the vehicle. Even though this industry is relatively new, there's no end to the kind of creativity that these owners are able to come up with!

If you've come to the conclusion that owning a gourmet food truck is a commitment that fits within your skill set and future career plans, we can start exploring in general, the types of food you might serve.

3 Square Meals A Day

The actual type of food you serve will often depend on the time of day you will operate or even your location. Breakfast is extremely popular but your menu has to be quick and simple because people are usually running late and in a hurry to get to work in the mornings. You're not going to be very popular if you make people late for their jobs.

Another great option for breakfast is to offer some items that don't have to be prepared like pastries, pre-packaged sandwiches, fruit and juices. Of course this goes against the whole concept of gourmet food trucks but it's still a good idea to have some of these items on-hand. Actually, all the preparation for these items can be made ahead of time and then loaded onto your truck for service. You're still preparing gourmet type foods but just not on your truck.

Next, lunch is the time of day where food trucks are most visible. Generally speaking, the lunch crowd has more time to wait for your freshly cooked meals. But even with the extra time, you will still have to serve food quickly if you want to keep your customers happy and coming back another day. And because lunch attracts so many customers to other trucks and restaurants, you'll have to offer competitive pricing in order to steer customers your way. One thing that helps is offering creative and unique food items that customers can't get anywhere else. This is what sets you apart from your competition!

Dinner is definitely another popular time to put your truck on the streets. You can serve customers coming to and from clubs, sporting events and concerts. As mentioned before, you need to keep the menu simple and offer dishes people can easily take with them. Obviously, evenings are primetime for attracting the dinner crowd. As a result, a number of so called "food truck pods" have formed in many cities to serve the dinner crowd. A food truck pod is a grouping of trucks that harness the power of multiple truck offerings to attract a larger attendance to the event. Food truck owners have observed that customers tend to purchase from more than one food truck at these events which is why mobile food owners are so eager to bring their trucks to these pods.

Tourists and special events are examples of two other venues where there are plenty of customers. Tourists are often attracted to local cuisine. Ideal locations are found near tourist attractions if you want to cater to this audience. You can also plan your location strategy around large events in your city. Get a calendar that lists events that are happening each month in your city so you can plan on getting the approval and permits to operate at those events!

Chapter 3 - Required Skills

Starting a food truck is a lot of work! While it does look like a lot of fun, building a successful food truck business takes a lot of planning if you want to increase your chances of success! And that doesn't mean just writing down some ideas, it takes significant planning. You'll need the right mentality as well as the right skills to survive in this industry. This relates directly to your ability to cope with stress and challenges... and rest assured there will be a lot of those challenging moments!

Starting a food truck means you're the boss. A goal most people strive for at one time or another. However, you'll need to be prepared to put in extremely long hours in the beginning. This is a critical period that will help set a good foundation for the future. Like a lot of industries, the food truck business is extremely competitive but lucrative.

Is The Market Saturated?

It's easy to think of the food truck industry as a new industry with relatively fewer competitors but you still need to act fast and start before your local market gets saturated. Los Angeles and New York have practically reached the saturation point. Smaller markets have fewer trucks but that is quickly changing.

The mobile food business is constantly experiencing growth and here are a few basic concepts you can follow in order to make good money in this industry. First of all, you should offer unique dishes not found anywhere else. As mentioned before, these could be unique variations of classic dishes. There's no need to reinvent the wheel here! One strategy is to offer lower prices than your competition. But many trucks are still very successful offering premium pricing on their menu items.

Finding the best locations definitely has an impact on how many customers you'll serve in a day. But as more and more trucks are hitting the streets, you'll have a harder and harder time finding good prime locations. And this goes almost without saying, you need to serve high quality food quickly!

As an entrepreneur, you need to be extremely organized and have the ability to make quick decisions. One example of quick decision-making is the ability to relocate if your current location isn't generating the type of income you're expecting. You will need alternate locations planned or be able to quickly get permits for other locations. Keep in mind that this is no ordinary job!

Running a food truck means you'll most likely be in several locations each week and run into unforeseen challenges at each and every location. This can take a huge toll on a person's stamina! While owning a food truck may seem easy to do on the surface... In reality, running a food truck is probably going to be one of the most challenging jobs you will ever have!

A Day in the Life of a Food Truck Owner

So what is a typical day like for a food truck owner? The beginning of the work day often starts several hours before the truck opens for business. If you're serving breakfast, you'll be up before the sun rises. Daily preparation often involves spending a few hours in the kitchen or out and about picking up ingredients.

After that, you'll need to load everything you need into your truck before heading out. Sometimes you'll have to deal with unexpected maintenance issues. If your truck or equipment malfunctions, your day could end before it even begins! At the close of the day, cleaning and organizing is the main priority before you repeat the process again the next day. This will be discussed in more detail in a later chapter.

Other tasks not directly related to the daily operation of your truck can include marketing, social media updates on Twitter and Facebook, managing staff, updating your website and billing. Running a food truck can be a tough job but certain background skills can come in handy when starting and running a successful food truck business.

A lot of the basic skills needed in any business will be helpful in this industry. Previous restaurant experience can definitely help, as well as a teaching or a business background. Being a self-starter is a good trait as well as marketing skills. To dive a little deeper into the subject, you're going to need to know your food. This includes:

The ability to recognize quality food
Assembling good food combinations
Good preparation techniques
Serving quality food fast and fresh
Pricing your food correctly

Don't over price or under price. It's a delicate balance but you can find your ideal price through testing.

Targeting Your Customers

You'll no doubt be deeply involved in the marketing of your truck and there are several aspects to successful marketing. Your menu needs to be aimed at your target audience. Because gourmet food trucks often serve niche items, customers can be well defined. A large part of food truck marketing involves free social media tools like Facebook and Twitter. Public relations can be another good method of marketing your business. Fundraisers are a great way to show that you are involved with your community.

Whenever you can, get on local TV and radio stations. This is free publicity that reaches a lot of people so get involved in events that can generate interest by the mass media.

Your food truck design is one of your most visible marketing elements so a great design on your truck can help you to be memorable. You'll also need an online presence as well. A great website can help current and future customers get to know you and your business. Don't forget to include a detailed "About" page that explains who you are and what your business is all about. And when you're out on the streets interacting with customers, don't forget to provide great customer service! People are going to remember you for that!

Answer questions from customers the best that you can. There are going to be a lot of people with diet restrictions. Like in any restaurant, they'll want to know what's in your food, or where your food comes from. There will be lots of other questions that we can't even predict! And of course you're going to get criticism about the customer's overall experience! No matter how good your food is or how well you treat your customers, there are going to be customers that are not happy. Accept constructive criticism and try to ignore irrational comments. Chances are you don't need those people as customers anyways. They probably complain about everything and nothing you do or say will change their opinion!

And one of the most important things to always keep in mind is to smile and be friendly! A good attitude can go a long way with your co-workers and customers!

Mechanical and Computer Skills

Aside from people skills, it's a good idea to have some basic mechanical skills also. Especially since your business depends on your truck's ability to get from location to location. There may be small repairs you can do yourself when last-minute emergencies arise. Other repairs you're guaranteed to experience are equipment breakdowns. Your grill might not light or your ice maker may decide to become a water dispenser instead. You never know when your equipment will fail and you need to be prepared to deal with it quickly or lose money.

You'll also be tested on your computer skills as well. Brush up on common computer problems either with your office computers or any computer-based equipment on your truck.

Among the essential skills needed to run a food truck is endurance. You need to be able to work long hours standing and working at a very fast pace... usually in cramped quarters and in extreme temperatures! This means you need to be in good physical shape. You also have to be mentally prepared for the stresses that come from the fast paced nature of the food truck business.

And last but not least, you will need patience. Keeping calm and in control of your emotions can help make solving problems a lot easier during the frenzy of your service. After going through the essential skills needed to run a successful food truck business, do you still think you can compete and survive this industry? Hopefully the answer is yes!

Chapter 4 - Top Reasons to Start a Food Truck

In this chapter, we're going to talk about business in general and then try to narrow down your own business goals when it comes to starting a food truck. First of all, you've heard all the great stories about how owning your own business will allow you to follow your dreams. A lot of times, this mean you'll have more creative freedom <u>and</u> you can pretty much set your own schedule.

The positive aspects are usually what drive people to get started. When you run your own business, it means that you are in complete control of your destiny and you get to reap the rewards of all your hard work. You will no longer be making someone else or another company rich. But along with the good, there also some negative aspects to running your own business.

On the negative side, YOU are still the individual who is in complete control and YOU are the one that must take full responsibility when things go bad. But let's dive a bit deeper and explore in more detail these positives and negatives. To start with, you should ask yourself "Why do I want to start a mobile food business?" We know almost every food truck owner has a different and unique answer but here are some of the more common reasons:

Be your own boss
Rewards for your own performance
Get away from the corporate world
Eliminate the 9-to-5 work day
More flexible schedule
Explore a passion
Potential to make more money
Ability to express yourself
Ability to control your career path
Develop untapped skills

No matter what the reason, new businesses are started everyday... some are successful while others are not. When starting out in the food truck business, one of the things you need to decide is whether you want to operate full-time or part-time? A lot of people who launch their own food trucks start out as a part-time business simply because they still work a full-time job.

Part-time or Full-time?

Running a food truck part-time can provide a good source of extra income. This can be achieved by working nights and weekends. However running a part-time food truck when you're already working a full-time job can be extremely exhausting. And there's a high possibility that you may not make enough money to be able to maintain your truck when only operating part-time.

One option that has worked for some that are still working a full-time job is to hire workers to run your truck on a full-time basis. This allows you to reduce your time commitment actually working in your truck. But even if you've hired help to run your truck, you'll still be extremely busy with other aspects of running this business. A key point to remember is that you need to keep expenses low and don't take on more than you can handle. Expenses can easily add up and you'll find yourself extremely overwhelmed.

The fact of the matter is that working nights and weekends can drain you both physically and financially! Imagine working a full-time job and then going home and then starting another job in the evening and on the weekends. This leaves you with very little or maybe even no time for friends, family or fun!

Food Truck Homework

If you decide that you're going to start a food truck as a full-time business, you're going to quickly realize that there's even more commitment of time, money and resources. When running a full-time food truck business (and this goes for part-time as well), you need to have everything fully researched. Your research needs to be completed way before you even buy your truck! I'll go over some of the things that need to be in your research. Consider this your homework. The following items are not meant to be comprehensive because some of it varies with your location or type of food you will be serving.

First, you need to learn the mobile food business inside and out. You have to live, eat and breathe food trucks for several months if you really want to learn how this industry works. To find out what makes the competition tick, you're going have to attend a lot of food truck festivals and try out of food from different trucks. Find out what they're doing. Figure out what works and what doesn't work.

If you want your truck to be successful, you're going to have to provide an excellent product if you want customers to return. There are lots of other trucks out there and your food has to be just as good or better to compete with established trucks which already have a huge following. You still have to work extremely hard to make your truck stand out! It may seem that I'm repeating myself on this but I want drive this concept home. Competition is fierce out there and you're going to have to go over-the-top if you want to survive in this business.

While the food truck business can make you feel like a star, there are other sides of the business that might make you want to crawl into a corner! You're going to need to obtain the proper permits and licenses before you can even serve your first customer! Knowing the local ordinances will also help avoid location problems which can lead to parking tickets or eviction.

Complying with health codes is an area of your truck that needs constant attention. Health inspectors need to approve your health and safety practices before you can start selling food. And while adhering to health codes is important, equally important are proper bookkeeping methods because you're going to need to know if you're generating profits or losses in your day-to-day operations.

Once you're ready to open up your business to customers, be ready to deliver quick quality food. And because you're going to be doing a lot of the same things every day, it's a good idea to set up a successful daily routine that can be easily followed. After all that, the biggest factor that will help skyrocket your success is to secure great locations in your area. Because there is so much competition out there you have to become creative when it comes to good locations.

Chapter 5 - Writing Your Business Plan

In this chapter, we are going to go over the actual steps of forming your food truck business plan. But first, let's define what a business plan actually is? In essence, a business plan explains in detail how you will operate your business. A good business plan helps you organize all aspects of running your business right from the very beginning! If you've never written a business plan before, you're not alone. A lot of people need help or are unsure of what to include in a business plan. Don't worry if you fall into that category! It's not that complicated!

Generally, a food truck business plan can contain a list of locations where you plan on parking to attract customers. A list of your food suppliers can also be included so you'll know exactly where your ingredients will come from. It's also a good idea to list alternate suppliers too! A business plan can spell out your source of funding. Most likely, funding will come from a bank but other methods can also be listed. You're also going to want to include estimates of what it will cost for you to start your business. Expenses for the first few months of operations can be included here as well. There can be other items you can add depending on your needs... however this is just a basic overview to help you get thinking about writing your business plan.

An important aspect of a business plan is that it's not locked in stone. Your business plan can be modified as your business grows and expands.

What to Include In Your Business Plan?

At this point you may be asking "What specifically needs to be included in a business plan?" The very first thing you need in your business plan is an executive summary. An executive summary is basically a brief overview of your business.

It actually explains the purpose of your business. It also explains what you want to achieve with your business. What are your future goals?

You'll want to do a competitive analysis as well. This will help you understand and know who your competition will be. Are there other trucks in your city that are serving the same type of food as yours? The competitive analysis can provide insight on what makes your competition so successful in your city or region. Proper analysis can help reveal the strengths and weaknesses of the competition. By knowing what your competition is doing you can adapt and do something better with your own truck. This can help you develop something new that the competition doesn't have.

In addition, you'll want to include your product offerings too. This includes a detailed list of your menu items. You may want to explain why you chose to put these items on the menu. Write down how your food will be prepared. This will also help you decide what type of equipment you will need. Your business plan will also include an industry analysis. In your case, you could explain the growing popularity of the food truck industry and why you want to be a part of it. The industry analysis should also explain how you'll compete with other food trucks in your area. You might also want to include any relevant facts and statistics about this industry in this section.

Another part of your business plan should include sales and marketing information. This will spell out your promotion and marketing plans. As part of sales and marketing, explain your social media strategy. This will include the development of your website which is an important marketing tool in and of itself. You should also document other marketing efforts such as e-mail marketing which has been used very successfully in other industries for years. You can also list locations, events, festivals and venues you plan on attending. When preparing your sales and marketing analysis, you should compare your prices against your competition's prices. Be as detailed as you can in your sales and marketing documentation.

Additional Business Plan Info

Moving away from sales and marketing, you'll also want to explain your management structure. Clearly describe the roles of the primary individuals so that there's no question of each person's duties within the business. You're also going to want to list out your day-to-day operations and explain how the daily tasks will be accomplished. For example, information listed in the day-to-day operations can explain where you will be preparing your food. This could be a commercial kitchen or directly inside the truck. Also in your daily operations, you should explain when and where you will buy your ingredients.

As part of your business plan, it is important to do some financial projections and include realistic information on how you plan to become profitable. These projections will help you estimate when you will become profitable by being able to pay off your startup expenses.

You're going to want to prepare a cash and balance sheet estimate for the first year so you know exactly where your money is coming from and where it is spent. When preparing your financial projections, don't overestimate your profit potential. All this information will help you determine your financial requirements so you can estimate how much financing will you need. The amount of financing needed is based on the information you entered for your profit and expense estimates.

Describe how and where you will invest your money. Please include how much of your own money you are going to invest, if any. Please take note that loans are more likely to be approved if you invest some of your own money. And you may want to include any other relevant documentation you feel will be helpful. This can include licenses, permits, awards and diplomas. And just to reiterate, it is very important not to exaggerate any figures or documentation in your estimates. Just remember to include any relevant information that clearly explains your operations and when you expect make a profit.

To help you build your own business plan, it might be helpful to research existing business plans in similar industries to get ideas on how to develop your own plan. Writing your business plan is the first building block of your business. Investors and financial institutions like banks will be looking closely at your plan to determine if you're worthy of financial help.

Chapter 6 – Menu Planning

Up until now, I've covered important topics like your business plan, marketing and time commitment. The next piece of the puzzle that goes into building a food truck business is the planning of your menu. As with the other aspects of building a mobile business, there are a lot of factors you need to consider when planning a good menu. Part of it will be determined by what you know how to cook. You might also want to consider using local ingredients when available. This is especially relevant if that is a theme for your truck and your brand.

You might want to do some research and find out what types of food are popular in your area. Every region is known for some type of food so a regional specialty could be a theme. Your menu can also be determined by the time of day will you be operating your truck. And there's a good possibility that the size your of your menu may determine the size of the vehicle you will eventually need. Before you decide on the dishes that will be included in your menu, you need to test your recipes over and over again until they are perfected.

Find Taste Testers

Have your friends and family critique your food. Or even invite a small group of unrelated individuals to get real, unbiased opinions. Take note of the favorite recipes and evaluate the comments. Then test again with a different group of people and include variations of those popular recipes that people have already scrutinized. This is a great time to perfect recipes and your menu... before you have a hard deadline to get your truck in operation.

It's critical that you and your staff are able to produce consistent flavors with every dish. You don't want the same dishes tasting different on different days. People will notice even slight variations of their favorite foods. So try to keep your menu simple! Your food should be easy to make in large quantities. When you're coming up with ideas for dishes, you can always turn to the classics like burgers, hotdogs, sandwiches, salads burritos or pizzas as mentioned before. But to stay true to the essence of the gourmet food truck industry, you have to take those classic ideas and add your own special touch or twist.

Classic Dishes Transformed

Here are a couple of real-life examples of how successful food trucks are taking simple food concepts and transforming them into unforgettable menu items. The Devilicious food truck in San Diego has taken grilled cheese sandwiches to whole new level. Some of their popular masterpieces include the butter poached lobster grilled cheese which includes lobster, melted cheeses, caramelized onions and oven roasted Roma tomatoes on sourdough bread. Another crowd favorite is their Seared Asparagus grilled cheese topped with goat cheese, brie, caramelized onions, tomatoes and the option of adding bacon!

The Fish Box in Miami also takes the sandwich concept and uses it to create a huge following. They have a classic called the Minuta which is a Cuban specialty sandwich. This popular sandwich contains fried yellowtail snapper (which includes the tail) and topped with tartar sauce, ketchup and onions stuffed between two Cuban rolls.

As you've probably noticed, food trucks are a great way to get high-end restaurant style food out on the streets. A huge menu is not necessary to be successful. But the size and number of items you offer can be determined by the size your truck, the number of employees you have, customer volume and the speed of preparation. No matter how many dishes you can prepare, just remember that quality is the most important factor that keeps customers coming back for more.

Another popular theme with food trucks is to serve dishes that combine various ethnic flavors. Marination Mobile in Seattle has a very unique concept on ethnic favorites. They serve kimchee quesadillas which includes Kalua pork, coleslaw, cilantro and jalapenos. They also have a variation of the classic taco with fillings like Kalbi pork, miso ginger chicken or tofu. And finally, they also have sliders. These are classic little palm-sized burgers but instead of beef, they use Kalua pork or spam.

And finally desserts are always popular classics. When planning your menu, remember not to limit yourself to breakfast lunch or dinner items. People enjoy desserts even after a large meal. Entire food trucks have been created based solely on desserts and have become very successful. Some of the classic desserts served in food trucks are cupcakes, ice cream, donuts and beverages.

Of course, when served from a food truck, those desserts are always given a makeover and transformed into a unique sweet treat! The Sweet Republic food truck in Scottsdale, Arizona is an excellent example of a gourmet dessert truck. They specialize in ice cream desserts with unique textures and often include sweet and salty combinations. Obviously, if you're only serving ice cream like Sweet Republic, you will most likely experience a drop in business during the winter months... but less so if you're in warmer climates.

Chapter 7 - Sourcing Ingredients

In order to cook great food, you need great ingredients. Where you get those ingredients can be a quest in itself! Thorough planning comes into play again for your ingredient list. Knowing what to purchase in advance can help you to become more cost effective and efficient.

Start by listing out the ingredients that are absolutely necessary for you to operate your truck. An important factor in building this list is figuring out how much food you can keep fresh and stored safely. Look at how much storage capacity you have in your truck or in an off-site kitchen. As general practice and to stay within safety guidelines, it's always better to run out of food than to sell food that has gone bad! Being able to judge the right quantities to purchase comes from experience. There are different variables in each and every truck so it can take some time to figure out how much you need to buy to prevent waste.

Here are some of the most common factors that will help you determine the amount of food you'll need every time you open for business. The day of the week can have a large impact on the number of customers that will visit your truck. The time of day can have an equal impact on the number of customers you'll be serving. Certain events may require more or less food.

Examples are large city festivals or private events. Your marketing efforts also have an impact on how much food you need to purchase because the better your marketing efforts, the more people will buy your food.

Where to Buy Ingredients?

So where can you go to buy your ingredients? Again, it varies between different regions and cities... but here are some suggestions. Most supplies can be ordered from wholesale distributors. But you can buy your food directly from manufacturers as well. Look to local suppliers too because they can often get you the freshest ingredients. Co-ops are also an excellent choice because you can combine your resources along with different businesses. This results in increased buying power that can save money.

Over the years, warehouse stores have become very popular for restaurant owners. Stores like Costco and Sam's Warehouse are the best examples of warehouse stores. In general mobile food businesses can use the same wholesale companies and suppliers as restaurants. But if you're just starting out and don't know where to find food distributors, a good place to start is to search on the internet for your area. In your favorite search engine, do a search for "wholesale food distributors" and then add your city after that search term.

Local Suppliers

If you're looking for local food suppliers, a good source of information is just to ask area restaurants. You'll find that most are willing to help out. A great place to buy fresh ingredients is from local farms, farmers markets and local fishermen. Sourcing food from farmers markets has become commonplace and it's actually a top selling point for today's food trucks. If you're using fresh, local ingredients, then you should emphasize that point as part of your marketing campaign.

Organic and healthy foods are always a crowd pleaser! Especially in current times because a growing number of consumers are more conscious about what they eat. However, using organic ingredients may result in higher costs that should be reflected in your prices. Research has found that health-minded people do not mind paying a little more for healthier, organic alternatives.

It's also a good idea to get to know your local farmers and growers. By building a relationship with them, you might be able to get some better or exclusive deals with them! In the end, you may need to use multiple suppliers to get all the ingredients on your list.

Saving Money with Co-ops

Similarly, co-ops are a popular option that <u>can</u> be a money saver. When you are part of a co-op, you'll be joining together with several similar businesses to buy in bulk. The end result is lower costs for everyone involved. Partners in a co-op don't have to be other food trucks. You can invite similar businesses to join with you or find an existing group to be a part of. If you're unable to find co-op partners on your own, you might want to get referrals from distributors or farmers. They may have some names of other companies that are trying to do the same as you.

Warehouse Stores

If co-ops aren't for you, then another popular option is shopping clubs. These are better known as wholesale warehouse stores. Among these clubs are Costco Wholesale, Sam's Club and BJ's Wholesale Club. If you're already a member of these clubs, you already know that there is an annual membership required to become a member and to purchase from the stores. As mentioned before a lot of restaurant owners buy from warehouse stores simply because it's so convenient and you can get large quantities at one time.

To summarize, you need good quality ingredients in order to prepare great food and there are several viable options for food truck owners. What works for one business may not be the best option for others. Again, experimenting with different food sources is the only way to know what is best for you. But it's not a set-it-and-forget-it task. In the course of your business, you'll most likely find that you'll change suppliers several times. That's just the name of the game!

Chapter 8 - Acquiring a Vehicle

Now it's time to talk about your truck because after all, it is an integral part of your business! Your truck is what differentiates you from brick-and-mortar restaurants and other mobile food businesses. But finding a truck to fit your needs can be like finding the right piece of real estate! The right truck for you is going to be determined by how many customers you plan to feed as well as the type of food that will be served. Your budget will obviously play a big part in the decision as well as the location you'll be operating in.

There are two major areas you need to examine when purchasing a food truck. You will have to look at the vehicle itself and you have to evaluate the kitchen area. Together, those factors can create wide range of costs. A food truck and cost anywhere from $15,000 to over $100,000! But why is there such a gap in price? Here are some factors that influence that number:

Buying new vs. used
Vehicle size
Onboard equipment
Retrofitting

If you're buying a used truck that needs retrofitting, you can realistically expect up to a year to complete! As a rule of thumb, it's always a good idea to estimate a longer completion time to avoid disappointment. After all, how many times have you heard a contractor say it'll take X amount of days but in reality, it took much longer than their promised completion time? On the other hand, a brand-new food truck can pretty much be ready to go into operation right off the lot. Start-up time is going to be a lot quicker with a new truck!

Advantages of New Trucks

There are a number of advantages to buying a new food truck. One advantage is that they can be designed exactly to your specifications. A new food truck will most likely meet all current vehicle safety and health regulations without retrofitting. Buying new also means you'll have a new vehicle warranty... much like you'd get when buying a brand new car. This can be reassuring if anything breaks. Obviously new trucks cost more than used trucks but, you get the advantage of starting up with all your equipment in prime condition! However, many mobile business owners choose to purchase used trucks mainly because of their lower cost.

Saving Money with Used Trucks

If you go the route of buying used, you should definitely have a trusted mechanic inspect the truck thoroughly just like you'd do when buying a used car. Most trucks have been used in harsh conditions and you need to be sure of what you're getting into before you lay down any money! When shopping for a used truck, there are some key issues you need to look out for.

The first one is engine reliability. This will directly affect your ability to get your locations. Another issue is the amount of interior space. You need to determine if it has enough room for your staff and the kinds of foods you want to cook. And just like buying a used car you need to look at the make, model, year and also the mileage.

If you're going to retrofit, you need to add the cost of retrofitting to the price of the truck itself to figure out the total cost. If the truck comes with existing equipment, do a proper inspection to see if it's in good working order. You may or may not have to replace it.

As an alternative, you could end up converting a non-food related vehicle into a food truck. When using a non-food related truck (such as a large delivery vehicle), you're going to have to do a total retrofit to turn this vehicle into a food truck. This is probably one of the most time-consuming methods of all!

Whether you're buying new or used, there are going to be some common concerns that will arise for both. One of the issues to ponder will be whether or not there is enough room for all your cooking equipment? Will the cost of the truck fit within your budget? Budget constraints always seem to be a recurring theme with any business.

Are You Qualified to Drive a Food Truck?

Another thing to consider is whether or not you can actually drive the truck safely? Have you ever driven a truck like this before? For most food truck owners, this will be the first time they've driven a vehicle in this weight classification. You will need to know the gross weight because trucks over 26,000 pounds requires a commercial driver's license to operate it. And wouldn't you know it? Obtaining a commercial driver's license (or CDL) is yet another item on your to-do list!

So when shopping for a food truck, you need to carefully plan and review all available options. Always remember that your truck is the center of your business and is the most visible aspect of it!

Along the way, you'll probably work with a food truck designer that can create a virtual floor plan of your truck. This will help you better visualize the interior space and arrangement of equipment. Like any construction job, your space requirements need to be accurately mapped out before actual work begins! Poor planning can and <u>will</u> result in costly mistakes!

Renting a Food Truck

Now that we've covered new and used trucks, I want to introduce you to one more cost effective option for prospective food truck owners. This option involves renting or leasing a food truck and it can save you a lot of money... Especially when you're just starting out! Renting a food truck is great for those who want to try their hand at mobile food but aren't sure they are ready to make this a permanent career. Realistic rental rates can be found around $2000 a month.

Some people actually plan on renting a truck when first starting out. Then when income goals are consistently met, they are ready to buy their own truck. Like any piece of machinery, you'll need to perform regular maintenance to keep it running because you can't make money if you can't get your truck to your customers.

Vehicle Storage and Parking

When it comes to storing and parking your truck, there are some strict requirements you'll need to follow. Most cities require that food trucks park at a Department of Health approved location when preparing food before or in the interim between services. But what types of facilities are approved? Here are some of typical food truck storage facilities:

Commissary
Commercial kitchen
Dedicated mobile food facilities

You'll need to check your local laws and regulations for overnight food truck storage as well. This is most likely a commissary. According to Mobile-Cuisine.com, the commissary is the lot that you're legally required to park your vehicle when not in use. It's against the law to store or prepare food, beverages or any food related items at a private home or unapproved structures. Commissary costs are paid monthly and could cost on average about $800 to $1200 per month. The rate varies because each commissary offers different types of features. They can include security cameras, 24-hour a day security staff, electricity and fuel or other necessary supplies.

Chapter 9 - Licensing and Regulations

Owning a food truck comes with its own set of laws and regulations. Specifically, I'm going to explain the areas of licensing and required permits. Some may find this process informative while for others, it can be a burden. I never said running a food truck was going to be all fun and games! All joking aside, getting your truck licensed and permitted is however an area where you'll need to pay particular attention to.

While it may seem like a hassle just to get your food truck on the road, the required health codes and regulations has actually helped the food truck industry really take off and grow! By requiring trucks to pass all health requirements, it allows customers to gain confidence when it comes to consuming meals from food trucks. But requirements can differ because every city, county and state has their own specific operating requirements.

Throughout the life of your food truck business, there are going to be some specific things that health inspectors will look for when they show up. This list is not comprehensive but it will give you a general idea of what you need to do to pass an inspection:

Proof of ownership
Use of an approved commissary
Proper sanitary practices
Proper food storage procedures
Food maintained at proper temperatures
Approved operating licenses

This is but a small list of items inspectors will check on in the operation of your business. During the course of your business, truck inspections will be conducted annually... and usually at random! So it's good practice to keep everything according code and to follow the rules. Any violations can bring on unexpected fines. And your business can be shut down if you have too many violations. The issues causing the shutdown must be corrected before you can re-open for business. Continued violations can lead to a permanent shutdown of your business. So it's really important to develop good habits right from the very start so things don't get out of hand!

Just to reiterate what we just learned. You'll need to follow all vehicle requirements. You need to stay as sanitary as possible. Keep all foods at the proper temperatures. And maintain proper ventilation inside your truck. Violations can create a bad reputation that can destroy your business in an instant! I can't stress this enough!

Additional Certificates and Legal Documentation

In addition to the obtaining the proper licenses and permits for your truck, there may be additional documentation you will need to file. Especially if you're operating your truck under a different name than what's listed on your business license. This can happen if you have an existing business but later open up a food truck under another name. If you are operating under different business name, you would need a Doing Business As (or DBA) certificate. This is legally required if you're conducting business under a fictitious name.

In most states, businesses need to register with the state tax agency and obtain certain tax permits as a seller. You'll also need an employee identification number (or EIN) which allows you to identify your business on government forms and documents. It's exactly like a social security number but this number is associated with your business. You'll most likely be assigned an employee identification number when you apply for your business license. An employee identification number is required whether you hire employees or not. If you have your business license but don't have an EIN, you can apply for one yourself at IRS.gov. The process is simple.

Protecting Your Personal Assets

When forming your business entity, you may want to consider incorporation. This will help protect your personal assets from liability. Incorporation helps you as the owner and as an individual. If someone gets injured because of your business, they'll sue your corporation instead of you and your personal assets. However incorporating doesn't mean you're 100% protected but it does effectively separate you from your business and provide an additional layer of insulation from your personal assets. One of the most common methods of incorporating is forming a Limited Liability Company or LLC. This option is great for small businesses. A couple of great resources online to learn about incorporation are at MyLLC.com and LegalZoom.com.

As with any important business activity, you should consult with a lawyer first to weigh your options before you proceed. Once you have all the legal paperwork taken care of, it's time to explore where you can park your truck to conduct business. When it comes to parking your truck you'll need to pay particular attention to city zoning and parking regulations. Areas of the city will be designated as commercial or non-commercial zones… In other words you can't just park anywhere you choose. Visiting with the County Clerk will provide you with a good list of approved parking locations. If you play by the rules, you'll avoid parking violations… at least most of the time!

When you're out on the streets, it's a good idea to build relationships with parking enforcement officers. They may be a bit more lenient for accidental violations if they know you. Just be friendly with them! And definitely pay attention to local ordinances. For example, in certain cities, a food truck may not park within X number of blocks from a school during school hours. As with everything, there also some unwritten rules when it comes to food trucks. Brick-and-mortar restaurant owners may not want food trucks parking in front of their businesses and "stealing" their customers.

So be wary of your surroundings. Just use some common sense when finding a location. Some cities like Chicago, by law don't allow food trucks to park within 200 feet of similar businesses. However that could change. It's often a good idea to build relationships with noncompetitive businesses and form a partnership that can be beneficial to both parties involved. This simple action can later translate to increased sales and customers you would not have gotten otherwise.

Chapter 10 - Spotting Good Locations

Getting customers to your truck is how you're going to make money in this business. Where you park your truck will have a huge impact on your success. And you'll need to know where you can legally park so you can effectively reach hungry customers. You may have even driven around and found some areas you think are perfect! But not so fast! The competition is probably already aware of that same location too!

As more and more food trucks hit the streets, it's becoming more and more difficult to find prime locations. And these days regulations and angry restaurant owners are making the quest for a location even more challenging.

But here is some practical advice to keep on hand. You want to find a few regular locations that work well for your food truck. Or find one great prime location that continually provides the best customer service base. Some examples of good parking locations include:

Shopping malls
Business parks
Tourist areas
Sports venues
Festivals and events
Conventions
College campuses
Parks and beaches
Car dealerships
And office parks

It takes time and resources to find the best locations. Plus you'll want to find a few other potential locations as a backup plan in case your regular spot is occupied that day. Even if you've found the perfect location that works, that could change because laws and ordinances may change over time. And remember different times of the year may affect your success in certain locations. Finding a great parking spot often requires on-location scouting and lots of driving around.

Reserving Your Locations

If you've found a spot that continually works, you may need a way to reserve your location on the days you want to park there. One way to reserve those prime locations is to use a staging vehicle to physically occupy the spot until your truck arrives. In extreme cases, you may need to park your staging vehicle the night before or very early in the morning to snag the spot!

If you are a new truck owner, please respect the other more established food truck owners that are already operating in the area you want to pursue. Some food truck owners may feel that you are invading their territory. But if you get to know them, you'll find that the food truck community is very respectful of other mobile food businesses. It may also be a good idea to meet with local store owners and neighborhood business associations to introduce you and your business before settling on the location.

Chapter 11 - Commercial Kitchens and Safety

Back in Chapter 8, I introduced the role of commercial kitchens in the food truck industry. Commercial kitchens are part of what helps keep this industry in-check and promotes overall safety. When you run a food truck business, you're going to spend a great deal time inside your truck. However you'll probably spend an even greater amount time inside a commissary or commercial kitchen. The reason you need a commissary is that it's illegal to prepare food at home to sell in your truck. Your truck and commissary need to comply with local health codes.

Staying Legal

As mentioned earlier, health inspectors will have to make sure that your food is stored and handled safely within your business. Failure to do so can result in violations which can cost you time and money.

If you own a restaurant, you already have a commercial kitchen. If not, you'll need to find a commercial kitchen or commissary to rent.

A quick online search can help you find a list of commissaries in your area quickly. Or you could go the old-fashioned way and search the Yellow Pages. Craigslist sometimes lists kitchen rentals. Or you can get referrals from other food related businesses. There are also some national directories that you can search through such as:

CommercialKitchenForRent.com
CulinaryIncubator.com

Commercial kitchens charge a monthly fee for usage but there are ways that you can reduce the cost of renting a commissary or commercial kitchen. One way to reduce costs is to share a commercial kitchen with another business. That way you can split the cost of the monthly rent. A requirement to rent a kitchen is liability insurance, however, each kitchen or commissary will most likely have additional requirements that are specific to them. Just be sure to ask what they are. If you have trouble finding a commissary, there are some additional options when it comes to renting kitchens.

Alternatives to Commissaries

Schools, churches or other organizations may have a certified commercial kitchen for rent. Other options include firehouses, hospitals and catering facilities. If you go with one of these options, you'll probably have to coordinate with the schedules of the kitchen owners. That's because you'll only have access to these kitchens early in the morning, late at night or whenever they're not in use. Thorough research can uncover a great deal on a kitchen rental.

When you've found a commercial kitchen you want to rent, make sure you get a contract in writing. That way everything is spelled out in case there are problems. The rules for commercial kitchens exist to protect the consumer and to promote cleanliness in the food truck industry. Never put your business at risk by taking shortcuts when comes to cleanliness. A clean and safe kitchen can help in your success by preventing germs and allowing you to operate safely.

Thorough cleaning should be a priority. And take measures to avoid food contamination. Daily cleaning tasks should be written down and followed religiously. Also be aware of expiration dates on packaging. Make sure doors on refrigerators and freezers close properly so that they can maintain their temperatures correctly... and never undercooked food!

Take the initiative. It's a good idea to stay persistent and conduct your own health inspections. In the end, you should be proud of your cleanliness and safety procedures... So will your customers!

Chapter 12 - Hiring Employees

As an entrepreneur, you will at some point need to hire employees. Unless you want to do everything yourself, you're going to need to hire help. It's just part of your duties as you grow and expand your business. In a food truck, some of the typical positions you might have open are:

Chef

Driver

Kitchen staff

Marketing specialist

Servers

And others

Once again, you need to do proper research before hiring any employees. Find out the compensation rates for the type of employees you want to hire. You need to know how much the industry is paying for the position you're posting so you can stay competitive and attract the best candidates. If you've never done it before, hiring employees can be a challenging task. But you're not alone! It can be challenging for people who do have experience with hiring also.

The first step in the hiring process is writing a job description. A good job description should concisely explain the work that needs to be performed by the employee. The job description should also detail the employee's expected responsibilities. Indicate whether this is part-time or full-time work. Also include the hours the employee will be expected to work. Does this position require nights and weekends? Don't forget to post the pay rate because this will help filter out unwanted candidates and narrow down your choices right off the bat.

Obviously, there are going to be certain qualities to look for in prospective employees. Some of the highly desired qualities are:

Cleanliness
Punctuality
Dedication
Work ethics

Now the next question I want to address is "Where do you find good employees?" There are several places you can start with. You can search in classified ads, Craigslist, scout talent in culinary schools, local bulletin boards, or just ask around and get word-of-mouth recommendations. As a small business owner, chances are you're going to be the one conducting interviews. This may seem like a frightening task but let's run through some of the things that will make the interview go smoother.

Conducting an Interview

First of all, you need to be prepared to conduct an interview and have your questions ready. Think about what you want to ask long before you call the first applicant. Have your questions printed out to use as an outline during the interview. Create a relaxed atmosphere during the interview. Make it conversational. It'll make you and your applicant feel more comfortable. Don't conduct your interview like an interrogation. Your goal is to find out their skills and strengths. Ask about their previous work experience. But don't ask personal questions.

You should definitely check out their references listed on the application. And a good employer always does background checks before hiring. Sometimes it may be a good idea to have current employees help determine if the new applicant is a good fit for your team. This can be done by simply introducing him or her to your staff and letting them talk to the potential new team member. It's also a good idea to give a tour of your truck and maybe even the commissary that you're working in. Give them a taste of your work conditions.

Once you think you have found the right candidate, the next thing to do is to hire them! Afterwards, send a nice thank you letter to the other applicants that did not get the job. Finding and hiring a new employee can be both exciting and nerve-racking! But the challenge doesn't end there. You are now responsible for that new employee when they're on the clock!

Responsibilities as an Employer

If you're new to hiring or have done it in the past, here are some simple reminders to follow as an employer. Listen to your employees. Communicate clearly to your staff. And don't abuse your position. As a business owner, you need to create some rules and policies so everyone knows what to expect. Make sure your rules and policies are clearly written and given to all employees. You must include information about sick days, vacation policies, accruals, overtime pay and other topics related to the job.

Be specific about topics related to termination, including drug and alcohol use. Make it known that certain behaviors are not welcome such as stealing, rude behavior, sexual harassment, tardiness or violence. Make your new employee feel like they're a part of your business. Make them feel welcome. Be open to their opinions and ideas on how things can be improved.

We're all human so just be aware that mistakes will be made! But instead of yelling at your employees, explain how to properly avoid the mistake if it happens again. And don't criticize or disrespect your employees. This creates an atmosphere where your staff may start to question their future with your company. Happy employees are more productive and will stay with you longer.

Employee Taxes

One more subject related to the hiring of employees involves taxes. The fact of the matter is that if you have employees, you're going to have additional taxes to pay. As an employer, you are required to withhold various types of taxes from your employees before they're paid. The three types of taxes that can be withheld are income tax, FICA and Medicare.

Other type of payments you will have to cover can include workers compensation and disability benefits. As a result, you need to keep detailed records of the taxes that have been withheld. You also need to keep records of when payments were sent to the IRS just so you have proper documentation in case you're asked to show proof.

Hiring a good accountant can help ensure that you pay your federal, state and local taxes on time. Your accountant can also help you keep track of all these payments properly. For more information about withholding and taxes, go to IRS.gov or you can call your local IRS office.

Chapter 13 - Marketing and Design

Luckily we live in an era where there are many cost-effective options for marketing a food truck. Because of advances in technology, advanced marketing techniques are easily practiced by all. In this chapter, you'll learn about the important concepts of marketing and promoting your business. This will have a direct effect on your brand, visibility and eventually your income. We already know that good food and great customer service are the foundations of your business. But that's not enough! You won't be selling much food if customers don't know your business exists.

Marketing and promotion are vital components in any successful business. And it's important to have your marketing plan developed early on. Often, the first step in marketing is choosing a name for your business. In this case it is your food truck. The food truck business is very competitive and picking a good name is the key. There plenty of good and memorable names out there. But it's up to your creativity to come up with a good one that fits your business.

Picking a good name can be difficult. That's when you can ask for help to find a clever name. You could turn to friends and family or hold a contest. Ask your followers on Facebook and Twitter or use your blog to ask for suggestions. However, if you use social media to find a name, just be sure to offer a reward to the person who comes up with the winning name.

Picking a Food Truck Name

Your company name can be descriptive or catchy. The issue with catchy names is that consumers won't necessarily be able to identify the theme or type of food served in a truck. Here are a couple of catchy food truck names from Phoenix, Arizona. See if you can guess their specialties:

Mamma Toledo's
Torched Goodness

Mamma Toledo's sells homemade desserts while Torched Goodness serves gourmet crème brulée. Were you able to guess the theme of those trucks from their names alone?

On the other hand, here are a couple examples of descriptive food truck names. There's no guessing what they serve:

Short Leash Hotdogs
Shine Coffee

The name of your food truck can have a large impact on your business. Before settling on a name, make sure that the business name you want is available. Check with the county clerk or the Department of licensing to see if your name is available and not already taken. Other places to find available names are at your Chamber of Commerce, the US Patent and Trademark Office or at the Thomas register. Again, do your research before registering a name. And it's a good idea to have two or three alternate names on your list so you can have a backup plan in case your primary name is not available. You may or may not know this but you will need a registered business name and tax ID number before you can open a business checking account.

Food Truck Design

Once you have a business name finalized, you can start to think about logo and truck design. Your truck is going to be the most visible part of your food truck business. So you want to hire a good designer with fresh, clean looking ideas. As you've probably noticed most food trucks have eye-catching designs and you need to be able to compete with creative colors and graphics to make yourself different. Consult with your designer and tell him or her that you want bright colors, bold lettering and a clean looking logo. It helps that your designs are recognizable from a distance.

Most truck designs are applied with a vehicle wrap. Painting is outdated and expensive. Vehicle wraps are extremely common in today's food trucks. With a vehicle wrap, any design can be applied on a truck.

Once the wrap is attached, your truck will serve as a roaming billboard and advertisement. Vehicle wrap designers can be found locally and on the Internet. And if you're working with a food truck manufacturer or builder, they can often provide vehicle design services as well.

Before hiring a designer you should get design examples and view portfolios from various artists before hiring them. If you like your designer, you can also use that same artist to design your menu. This helps create a consistent look.

Renny's Oki Doki Okinawan Food Truck took a different approach. The owner had a childhood friend that just happened to be one of Disney's top animators. Knowing this, Renny Braga enlisted the skills of his talented friend to create a one of a kind design for his truck. I'm not necessarily saying you can get a Disney artist to design your truck but you may know some talented designers that could do the same for you!

All these elements will contribute to the overall branding of your food truck. Once you get rolling, you can consider putting your designs on cups, napkins, coasters business cards and other stationary. Your designs can create an ambience and overall atmosphere around your brand.

Once you have your logo and branding, it's time to move on to social media to help promote your business. Just about every mobile food business uses social media to market their truck. The top two services that truck owners use are Twitter and Facebook.

Tweeting Your Way to Success

If you're new to Twitter, here's what it is. It's a social networking and micro-blogging platform that allows status updates of up to 140 characters. Twitter is free to use and the more followers you have, the further the reach of your messages. Twitter provides real-time updates for you and your customers.

You'll be using Twitter to announce your location, specials, new items and other important messages. Twitter can also support two-way communication so you can respond to your followers through direct messages. It's also good practice to respond to Tweets directed to you to keep your customers engaged.

However it's not necessary to respond all tweets. But giving some response will show that you care about your customers.

When you're getting started with Twitter, you'll need a username, e-mail address and come up with a password. For people to recognize you, come up with a creative username. This is usually the name of your truck. It might be a good idea to search Twitter to see if the username you want is available. Actually, you should do this when you are first coming up with names for your truck. Once you have a Twitter account set up, you'll want to upload a profile image. It's a good idea to use your logo or a photo of your truck.

Facebook Status Updates

The other popular social network that truck owners are using is Facebook. For those who don't know what Facebook is, it's a social networking platform that allows status updates through text, images and video. Unlike Twitter, Facebook doesn't have a 140 character limit when typing updates. But similar to Twitter, Facebook is free to use. The goal on Facebook is to get "Likes". Getting "Likes" is similar to gaining followers. And the people who have "Liked" your Facebook page will instantly get all your updates in their account.

To use Facebook for your business, you need a business page or a fan page. If you already have a personal Facebook page, you can easily create a fan page. However we don't recommend using your personal page for your business status updates. It's a good idea to keep your personal updates separate from your professional business. Once you're all set up, start using Facebook to update your locations, menu items, share photos, videos and more!

And whenever you can, encourage people to "Like" your page. When people "Like" your page, they are essentially subscribed to all your updates. And updating your Facebook status frequently is important for engagement. Once your social media accounts are set up, you'll want to promote your Facebook and Twitter profiles everywhere! This information could printed be on your truck graphics, business cards and on your website.

How to Start Your Website

The next step in promoting your business is to create a website. Having a website is equally as important as using social media. A website is essential for any business whether it's an online or offline business.

And a good web designer or developer can develop a complete website for you. As with logo designers, you should view sample websites from the web designer first before hiring them. Sometimes the term web designer and web developer can be used interchangeably.

To start a website you're going to need a domain name and a hosting account. Your domain name is your website address. An example would be www.yourfoodtruck.com. A hosting account is where your website files are stored and accessed by visitors… kind of like a remote hard drive or computer.

But let's take a step back before building your site. First you need to see if your domain name is available. Again, it is helpful if you come up with a domain name when you are picking a business name. But once you've decided on your domain name, you'll need a hosting provider such as Bluehost. Bluehost actually gives you a free domain name that you own when you host your website with them.

But here's a website building tip that can save you a lot of money. Don't pay a web designer or developer to build your website! You can build the website yourself without any experience! It's easier than you think! You can simply buy hosting and the domain yourself. Then install Wordpress to manage your website. You may or may not know what Wordpress is, but it's an extremely popular blogging platform that's free and easy-to-use.

A large percentage of food truck websites use Wordpress as their preferred management platform. And the best thing about using Wordpress is that there are thousands of free Wordpress themes that you can use to customize the look of your site. With so many themes available, you can change the look your site instantly without the help of a web designer. With Wordpress you can easily create any and all pages yourself such as the Homepage, About Us, Contact Us and Menu pages. And let's not forget the original function of Wordpress which is its incredible blog capabilities.

And even if you don't choose to create your website yourself, a designer would probably use Wordpress anyways! So why pay them for something you can do on your own! At the very least, buy your hosting and domain name yourself before turning it over to a web designer or developer. They'll probably charge you a set-up fee for the initial work with your hosting account! You can easily set up Wordpress yourself through the hosting control panel. Almost every hosting provider makes it easy with one-click Wordpress installs. So why pay a designer for something you can do yourself? People with literally no web building experience have built beautiful websites with Wordpress.

This is just an overview of some of the marketing strategies that need to be employed by food truck owners. If you want a complete food truck marketing plan, the next book in this series called The Food Truck Marketing Handbook explains in detail the tools and effective strategies that will help build a strong social media following including tactics not found anywhere else. It is completely tailored to the food truck owner.

Chapter 14 - Expenses and Cash Flow

Starting a business is expensive and you need to know how to cover your start-up costs before you can get your food truck idea off the drawing board and onto the streets. There's no doubt that menu planning and designing your truck are considered the "fun" aspects of this business. While it can also be fun running a food truck, just remember that it is still a business and should be treated like one. Looks can be deceiving but starting a food truck business is just like starting a regular restaurant except for the mobility and lower start-up costs. It's definitely not a get rich quick business! It takes long hours and dedication to make it and survive in this industry.

To be successful, you need to watch your cash flow. This is achieved through proper pricing and smart supply purchases. In addition, you need to keep a close eye on expenses. There are no set costs for starting a gourmet food truck business. Each food truck is unique and has different requirements. Start by making a list of all the expenses you can think of. Don't be surprised if your costs add up fast. You'll need to calculate how much it costs to produce each dish. This is important because in the beginning, you need to get a good idea of the amount of money needed to start and maintain your business. And don't forget legal, accounting and other financial expenses.

Operating Expenses

Another part of the equation is operating expenses. Operating expenses are the ongoing costs that keep your business running. You can consider operating costs like recurring monthly payments. Breaking it down even further gives us fixed and variable expenses. Examples of fixed expenses can include commissaries, vehicle payments, vehicle rental, website hosting and insurance. When it comes to variable expenses, ingredients, fuel, repairs, marketing and special permits can fall into this category. It's important to be able to estimate your costs each month as accurately as possible. And you might need to anticipate a little extra for the unknown. Unexpected costs can come from the last minute events or vehicle repairs.

Keep in mind that it's going to take time for your business to become profitable. And it can be hard to watch money fly out the door without any return on investment in the early months. Obviously, the bigger your initial investment, the longer it will take to pay it back. One advantage of a food truck is that it has lower overhead costs. However you'll still need enough capital on-hand to be able to continue running for at least six months to a year in the beginning. Studies have shown that it often takes businesses at least two years to start showing profits. For most people, that is an eternity!

Managing Food Volume

You'll need to effectively manage the volume of food. Here are the variables that help determine volume. Part of it is how much food you will buy and how much of it you're going to prepare. Then you'll need to figure out how much you're going to sell. Calculating volume can be difficult. You can estimate your volume in the beginning to get a ballpark figure but only experience will make you better at estimating how much to buy and prepare.

The ongoing dilemma is figuring out how much food to bring to a service. This depends on how much you think you can sell. Often you won't know until you run out of food. And when you do run out of food, you won't know how much food you could've sold! This can be very frustrating.

The other challenge is that you only have a limited time to sell your food because you're not open all day like a traditional restaurant. You need to be able to serve foods quickly and increase volume. Another aspect that comes into play is pricing your menu correctly. There needs to be balance in your pricing. If your prices are too high you won't sell much food. If your prices are too low, you won't make any money. On average, most food truck items are priced between $6 to $10 but some charge more.

Building Loyal Customers

To build a strong following for your truck, you need to have affordable prices. You can compare the prices of similar items from your competitors. Charging the right price is another skill that comes from experience. Your location plays a factor in determining what your customers will want to pay. Pricing in one city will be different than in another city. Portion size helps determine your price also.

You need to identify what makes your food different from the competition. If you charge much higher than the competition, then you need to justify why it costs more. Your customers will want to know.

Here are some reasons that you can charge more for your food than your competitors. You might be using organic ingredients, or maybe you're including side dishes not offered by your competitors. Your portion size may be larger. Maybe you're using imported ingredients. Serving a gluten-free menu can also justify a higher price. The bottom line here is that if you're spending more than you are making, then adjustments will have to be made.

Adjustments you can make are lowering supply costs, getting bulk discounts for your ingredients, adjustments to employees and staff size, you could join a co-op or you could improve your marketing strategies. When you've calculated your costs, determine how many items you need to sell just to break even. The first year is going to be the most difficult to become profitable! The first year is also where the most adjustments will be made. And of course there'll be some factors that are out of your control like:

Bad weather
Event cancellations
Health issues
Vehicle breakdowns

It's all part of business and every industry is faced with the same hurtles. Having lots of patience can go a long way to get you through the toughest parts of the start-up process.

Chapter 15 - Generating Startup Capital

Startup capital is the necessary ingredient that will literally get your business off the ground. Without it, your ideas will just remain on paper. But how much do you need? After you've determined your costs, you can start to calculate the amount of startup capital you'll need. As a general rule, it's safe to say that you'll need at least six months of funds on hand to get started. But you might want to get additional funds in case business starts off slow in the beginning.

For example, you may have figured on $27,000 in startup costs. Then in the next five months, you determined that you need $3300 per month to keep operating. Adding it all up, you're going to need a total of $43,500 in the first six months just to be able to stay open.

That's $27,000 + $3300 x 5 = $43,500

I know this is just a simple math problem but whatever you come up with for total startup capital, it's still a good idea to have some extra cash on the side. You might want to get financing for at least 20% more than you calculated for the first six months.

You'll also want to estimate your future income growth, but keep your long-term financial predictions realistic. Going back to your business plan, it should project your profits for up to five years. It should also explain how you plan to make this growth happen. Predictions can be presented monthly, quarterly or annually. Examples of future growth plans include menu additions, new marketing strategies, adding more locations or attending more venues.

Funding Sources

Lenders and investors want to know if they'll get reimbursed for lending you the money. Finding investors is not difficult but actually getting your hands on the startup capital can be a different story. One of the first places to look is your personal savings. Do you have enough money to start a business with your own bank account? If you don't, you could look to borrowing money from friends and family. While this can work, it can also put a strain on the relationship. While most will be supportive, you need to make sure that they are totally onboard with you.

Borrowing from friends and relatives sometimes results in a type of partnership. If this is the case, you need to clearly define the roles of each partner. Document each partner's responsibilities in writing. And let your lawyer draw up the legal documents and have all the partners sign it. Having everything properly documented helps avoid questions and conflicts in the future. Clearly indicate how each partner will be reimbursed for their contribution. If the money is a gift, state that in writing.

Also plan for what will happen what if a partner decides to drop out.

Perhaps the most common source of funds for small businesses comes from banks or credit unions. You'll need a good credit rating to prove that you can pay back the loan. It's recommended that you find out your credit score first before applying for a loan. You can find your credit score at one of the three main credit reporting agencies online at:

Equifax.com
Experian.com
Transunion.com

When you get your report, look for any errors and have them corrected before applying for the loan if possible. And it's always a good idea to invest <u>some</u> of your own money, even if you're applying for a bank loan.

Startup Funds from Crowdsourcing

A relatively new source of funding comes from a technique called crowdsourcing. Crowdsourcing is the practice of generating resources from the masses, with each person or organization contributing a small amount. Those small amounts add up and become large contributions that help you accomplish a task. Right now the most popular crowdsourcing website is Kickstarter.com. Kickstarter is a bit like a social media platform where you get to present your business plan in the form of text, images, video and social media. To get funding, it's almost as easy as specifying an amount of money you need and explaining to readers why you need the money and how it will be used.

KICKSTARTER

One of the requirements of Kickstarter is that you have to specify a deadline of when you want to reach your goal. This is usually between 1 to 60 days. You need to tell a persuasive story of who you are and how the funds are going to help get your business started. And once you can get your Kickstarter campaign started, share it with everyone! Use social media to get your message out to the masses. Get as many contributors as you can! You can even offer rewards for different contribution levels. This is used to entice backers to contribute predetermined amounts that could be as little as $5 to $500 or more!

Kickstarter is all or nothing funding. What that means is that you need to reach 100% of your financial goal by your set deadline or you will receive no money. However, if you reach the deadline and you are successful at reaching 100% or more of your funding goal, then you'll be well on your way to securing the startup capital you need. And the best thing is that you don't have to pay the money back! It's almost like a free loan! Only a small percentage of the total is kept by Kickstarter and you keep the rest.

When it comes to generating startup capital, there are plenty of options. You can use one method or even all of them to get the amount you need. Once you've got the money in hand, you're well on your way to starting your food truck venture!

Chapter 16 - Exit Strategy

In the final section, I'm going to talk about a subject that no one wants to talk about and that's ending your business! According to successful business owners and corporations, it's a good idea to have an exit strategy to expedite the process of getting out of a business. No matter how much you enjoy it, at some point, you <u>will</u> be getting out of the food truck business. So let's explore some of the options available to you.

Selling a food truck is common in this business and there are plenty of reasons why. Some people get burned out working in this fast-paced industry. While others become successful enough to open up a traditional brick-and-mortar restaurant and never hit the streets again. And some may even move to related industries like hospitality, food distribution or even food truck event planning. No matter what the reason, you may need a way to get out of this business quickly.

2 Ways to Get Out

There are two common ways to exit. The first is to sell your truck on its own or you can sell your business as a whole. Selling a truck means selling the vehicle and all the equipment inside it. This is practically the end of your business. It will no longer exist after this. On the other hand, if you sell your business as a whole, you actually sell your brand and culture along with the vehicle and all the equipment involved. This means your business can continue on with new owners under the same name if they choose.

Selling as a business allows the new owners to start off with a strong, existing customer base. If you sell as a business, you'll get a higher return than just selling off the equipment. To sell your entire food truck business, you need to determine the total value of the business as a whole. You need to prove the value of your business with accounting records from the last six months as a minimum. Prospective buyers may want to see records that date further back.

Some of the suggested items to include are things like ongoing expenses, sales figures, equipment, your receipts, any special contracts, permits and recipes. Setting your sales price can be a little bit of a challenge but here are some general guidelines. You'll need to consider tangible and non-tangible items in your price determination. Tangible items like your vehicle and equipment are easy to calculate a value while non-tangible items are harder to place a value on.

Here are some examples of non-tangible items:

Recipes
Reputation
Food quality
Branding
Loyal customers

Those (and more) all fall into the non-tangible category. Just keep in mind that your business is worth a lot more than just your vehicle and equipment. It's also important to let your potential buyers know if the businesses still in debt. If buyers see an easy way to get into your business, you're more likely to sell faster. It's also a good idea to provide after sales support to teach the new owners how to prepare your recipes and use your equipment.

Announcing the Sale of Your Business

Getting the word out to buyers is easy. You can post your business for sale on Craigslist, newspapers, on eBay, your Twitter and Facebook accounts, your website or any other specialized food industry marketplace. So what happens after you've sold your truck and business? It's common for a lot of people feel a sense of loss after they've sold their business especially if they've spent a lot of time and money building it.

Feel good after the sale that you were able to accomplish a dream you always wanted to try or at least be happy that you were able to leave this industry to move onto the next step in your career!

In conclusion, there are a lot of detailed aspects to running a mobile food business. Each truck is going to be different with different requirements. But no matter what, you should enjoy what you're doing. If you do something you love, it doesn't feel like work! Don't expect to get rich... Although that is entirely possible! But do expect a lot of work!

Final Thoughts

Remember to keep everything clean and sanitary. And most of all have fun! This is your business so build it exactly the way you want. No one can run it better than you! So get out there and cook some street food!

You can always find out the most current information about starting and running a food truck at:

FoodTruckBusinessPlan.com

The site is regularly updated with new content and new tutorials so check back often. And thank you for making time to read this guide on how to start a food truck business! Get out there, make friends with the community and have fun!

Resources

Find a Commissary or Commercial Kitchen

CommercialKitchenForRent.com
CulinaryIncubator.com

Tax and Business Information

IRS.gov
MyLLC.com
LegalZoom.com

Food Truck Insurance

InsureMyFoodTruck.com

Website Resources

Bluehost.com
Wordpress.org
Twitter.com
Facebook.com

Crowdsourcing Funds

Kickstarter.com
Indigogo.com

Current Food Truck Information

FoodTruckBusinessPlan.com
Mobile-Cuisine.com

Would You Like to Know More?

Learn more about the food truck industry and what it takes to start your own food truck business with the other titles in the Food Truck Startup series.

The best part is that I frequently run special promotions and discount my books (usually $0.99 USD). It's a great way to save and learn about this unique career path.

The best way to get notified of these deals is to subscribe to my Entrepreneur's Book Club. It's free to join and you'll also get a copy of **Food Truck Vehicles and Equipment**. This free guide will introduce you to some of the components and systems found on food trucks as well as details on the actual vehicles.

Please visit the following URL to get promotion updates and download the free book:

TheFoodTruckStartup.com/free

Did you like this book?

I'd like to say thank you for purchasing my book. My goal is to provide the most complete information about food trucks and the industry. I hope you enjoyed it!

As a favor, I would be grateful if you could take a minute and please leave me a review for this book at the website you purchased it from. Your feedback will help me to continue writing and updating the information about the food truck industry.

Thank you!

Andrew Moorehouse

Blog: FoodTruckBusinessPlan.com

Books: TheFoodTruckStartup.com

Made in the USA
San Bernardino, CA
25 September 2015